PIANO SOLO

CALMING PIANO SOLOS

ISBN 978-1-70514-713-9

HAL•LEONARD®

For all works contained herein:
Unauthorized copying, arranging, adapting, recording, internet posting, public performance,
or other distribution of the music in this publication is an infringement of copyright.
Infringers are liable under the law.

Visit Hal Leonard Online at
www.halleonard.com

World headquarters, contact:
Hal Leonard
7777 West Bluemound Road
Milwaukee, WI 53213
Email: info@halleonard.com

In Europe, contact:
Hal Leonard Europe Limited
1 Red Place
London, W1K 6PL
Email: info@halleonardeurope.com

In Australia, contact:
Hal Leonard Australia Pty. Ltd.
4 Lentara Court
Cheltenham, Victoria, 3192 Australia
Email: info@halleonard.com.au

CONTENTS

AUTUMN COMES WINTER

By DAVID LANZ
and KRISTIN AMARIE LANZ

Copyright © 2016 by Lanz Music (BMI) and Amarie Music (ASCAP)
All Rights Reserved   Used by Permission

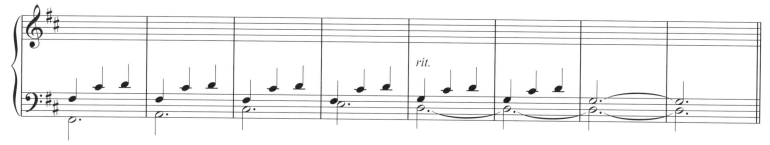

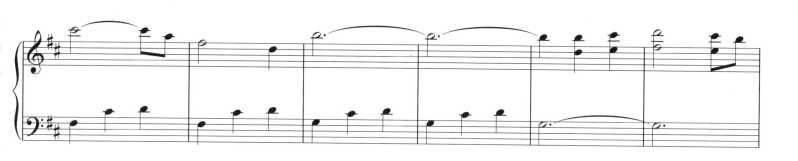

1st x only

To Coda ⊕

dim.

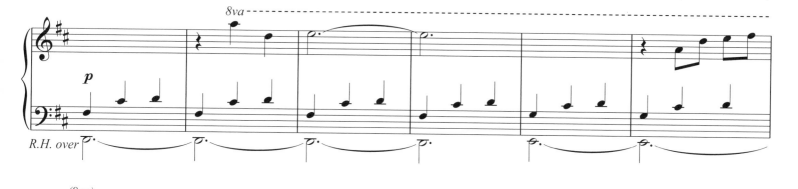

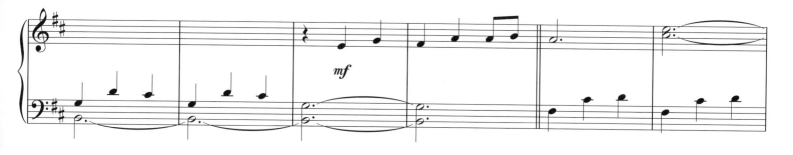

D.S. al Coda

CODA

dim.

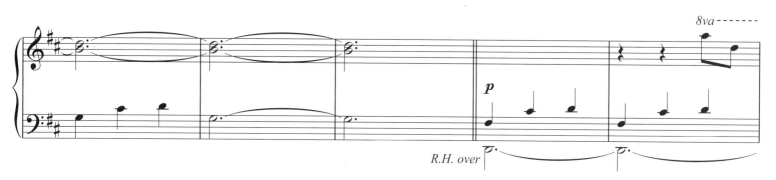

8va ------

p

R.H. over

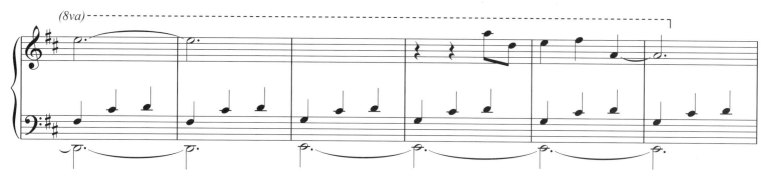

(8va)

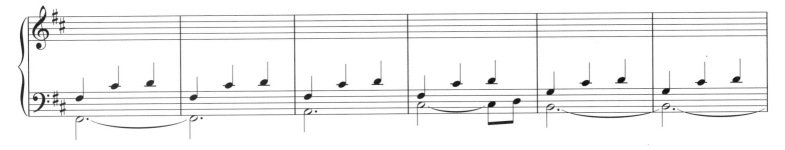

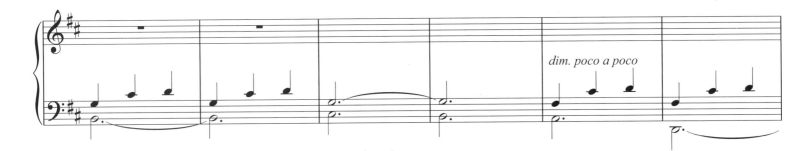

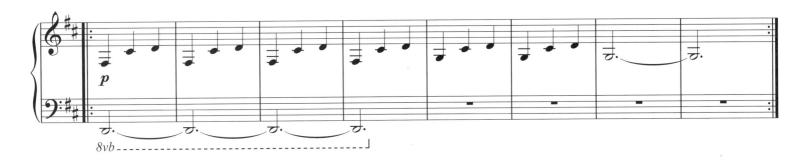

THE APPROACHING NIGHT

Composed by
PHILIP WESLEY

Copyright © 2008 Philip Wesley
All Rights Reserved   Used by Permission

8vb

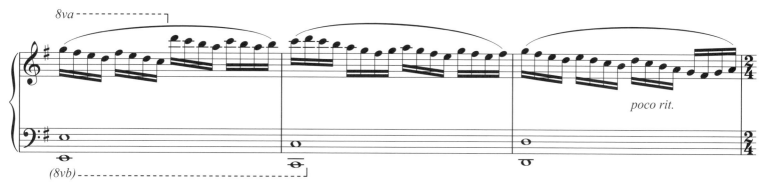

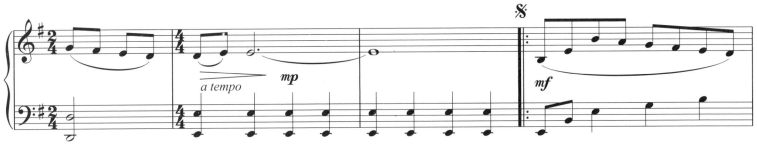

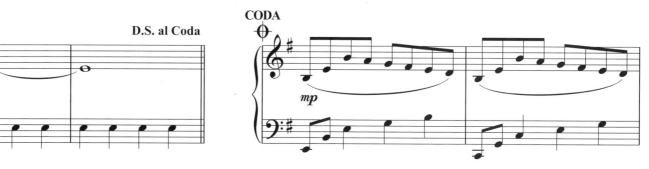

A BEAUTIFUL DISTRACTION

Composed by
MICHELE McLAUGHLIN

Copyright © 2015 Michele McLaughlin Music (ASCAP)
All Rights Reserved
Unauthorized duplication, sharing, copying or selling is a violation of applicable laws.

Poco più mosso

Lento

Poco più mosso

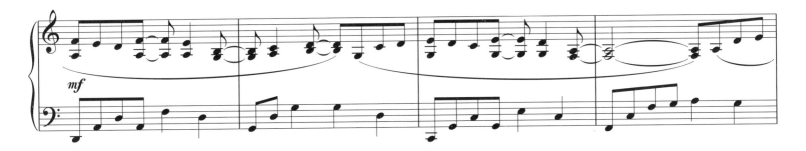

BEAUTY OF LIFE
(Piano Version)

Written by
GABRIELLE AAPRIE PETERSON

Moderately, expressively

Copyright © 2013 CD Baby Alpha Music
All Rights Reserved   Used by Permission

To Coda ⊕

rit.

a tempo

D.S. al Coda

CODA

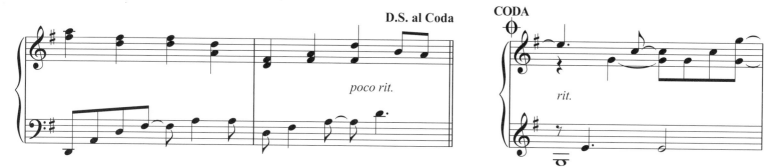

poco rit.

rit.

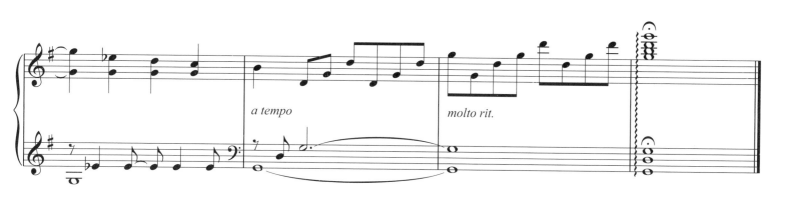

a tempo

molto rit.

BLUEBIRD

By ALEXIS FFRENCH

Tenderly (♩. = 50)

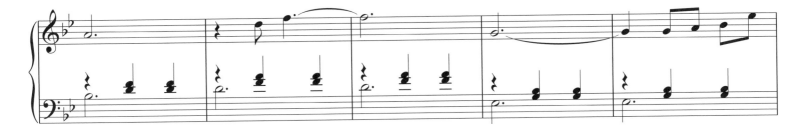

Copyright © 2018 UNIVERSAL MUSIC PUBLISHING LIMITED
All Rights in the U.S. and Canada Administered by UNIVERSAL - POLYGRAM INTERNATIONAL PUBLISHING, INC.
All Rights Reserved   Used by Permission

A CELTIC DREAM

Composed by
MICHELE McLAUGHLIN

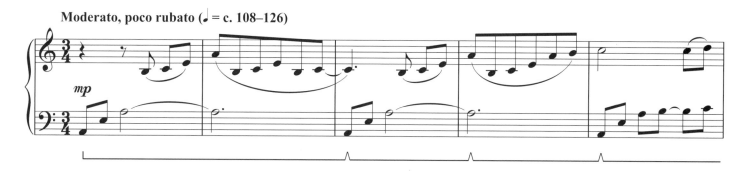

Copyright © 2019 Michele McLaughlin Music (ASCAP)
All Rights Reserved
Unauthorized duplication, sharing, copying or selling is a violation of applicable laws.

Poco più mosso (♩ = 144)

BUTTERFLY WALTZ

Written by
BRIAN CRAIN

(♩ = 132)

Both hands 8va throughout

Courtesy of TuneCore Publishing o/b/o Brian Crain Publishing
All Rights Reserved   Used by Permission

34

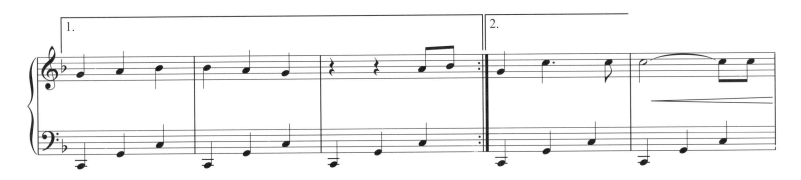

A CATALOGUE OF AFTERNOONS

Composed by
MAX RICHTER

Copyright © 2018 Mute Song Limited
International Copyright Secured   All Rights Reserved

CITY LIGHTS
from NIGHT

Music by
OLA GJEILO

Copyright © 2019 Chester Music Limited.
International Copyright Secured   All Rights Reserved
Used by Permission

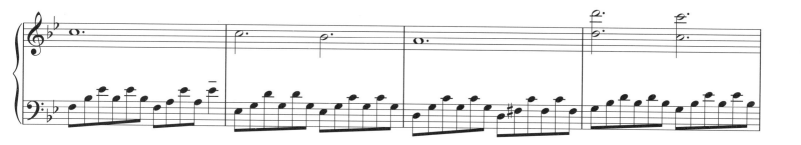

EARLY MORNING RANGE

By GEORGE WINSTON

Copyright © 1991 Dancing Cat Music
This arrangement Copyright © 2020 Dancing Cat Music
All Rights Reserved   Used by Permission

FLY

Music by
FLORIAN CHRISTL

Andante cantabile con moto

Copyright © 2018 Edition Sony Classical And Jazz
All Rights Administered by Sony Music Publishing (Germany) GmbH
International Copyright Secured   All Rights Reserved

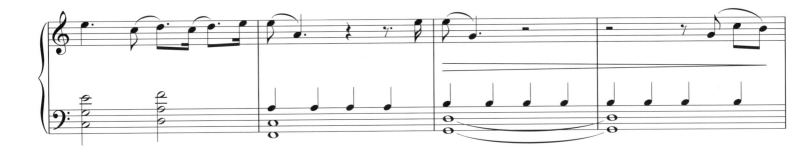

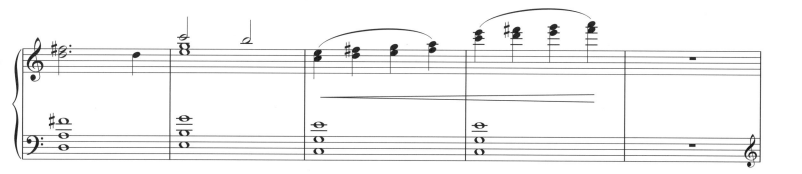

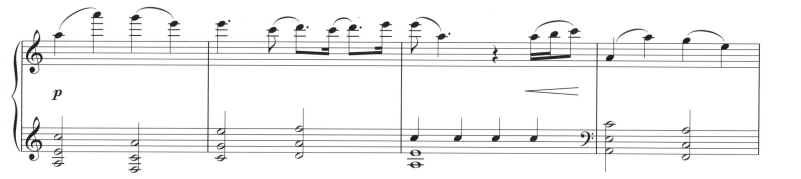

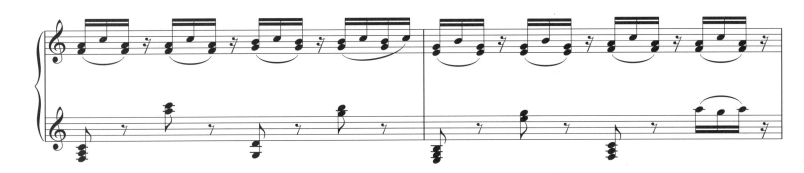

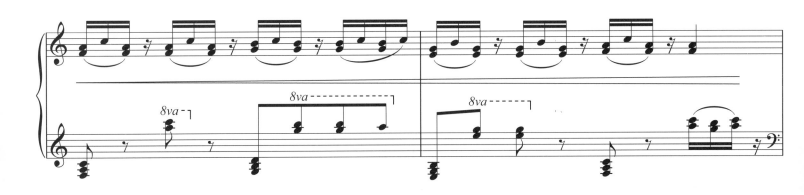

FRACTURE

By STEPHAN MOCCIO

Moderately, with freedom and a fragile heart

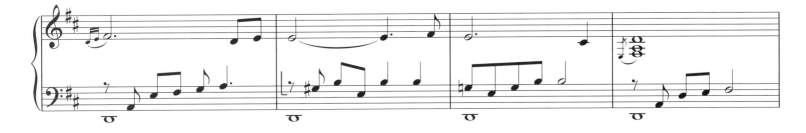

Copyright © 2020 SING LITTLE PENGUIN
All Rights Administered by SONGS OF UNIVERSAL, INC.
All Rights Reserved   Used by Permission

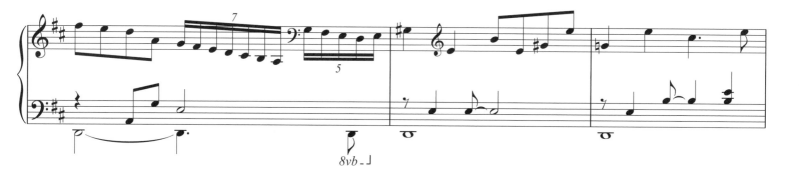

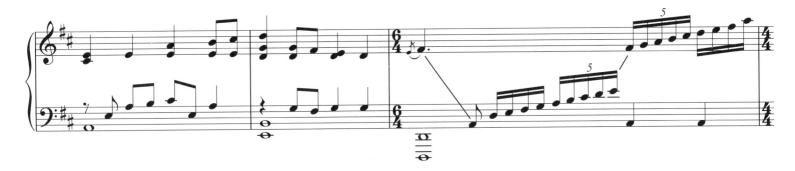

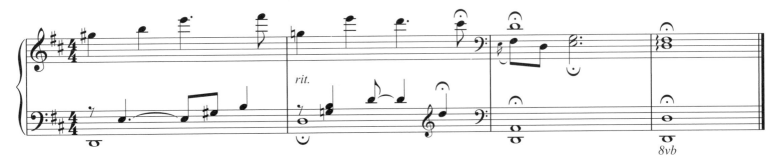

8vb

MELANCHOLIE

Music by
FLORIAN CHRISTL

Wehmütig getragen

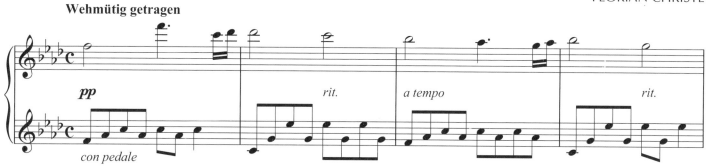

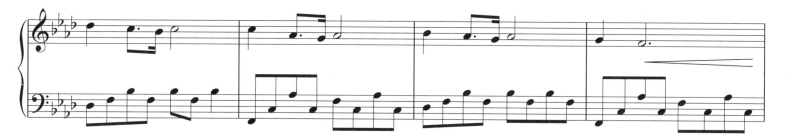

Copyright © 2020 Edition Sony Classical And Jazz
All Rights Administered by Sony Music Publishing (Germany) GmbH
International Copyright Secured   All Rights Reserved

THE GROWING SEASON

By PAUL CARDALL

Moderately slow, freely

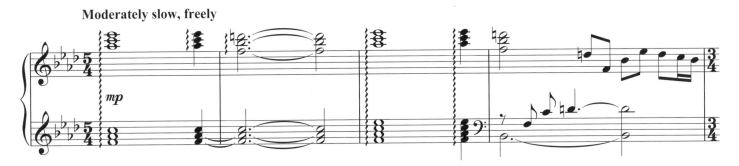

Copyright © 2019 Anthem Music Publishing I and Worth Of Souls Publishing
All Rights Administered by Anthem Entertainment
All Rights Reserved   Used by Permission

Moderately, expressively

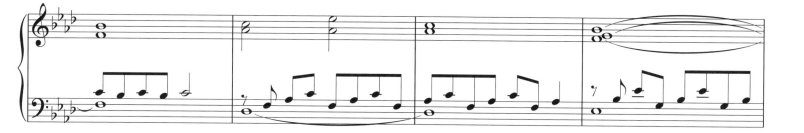

54

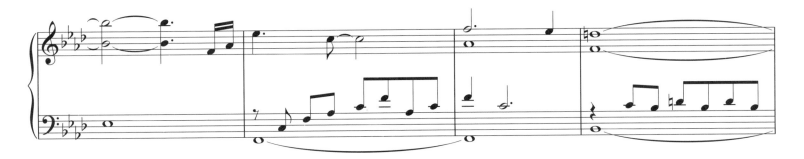

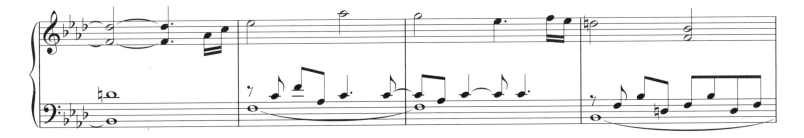

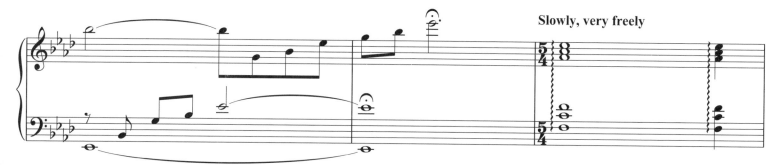

Slowly, very freely

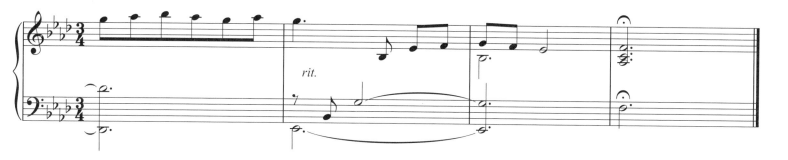

I GIORNI

By LUDOVICO EINAUDI

© 2003 FONIT CETRA MUSIC PUBLISHING SRL
All Rights in the U.S. and Canada Administered by WC MUSIC CORP.
All Rights Reserved   Used by Permission

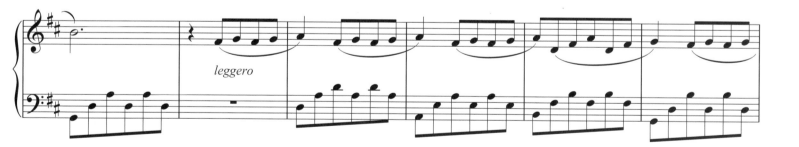

To Coda $\oplus$

pp *sognante*

una corda

D.S. al Coda

tre corde

CODA

pp *delicato*

una corda

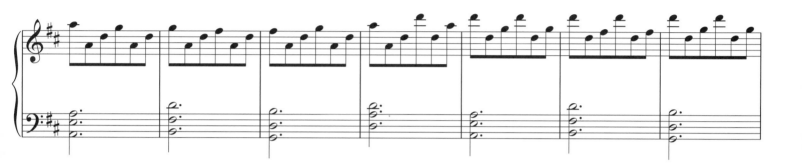

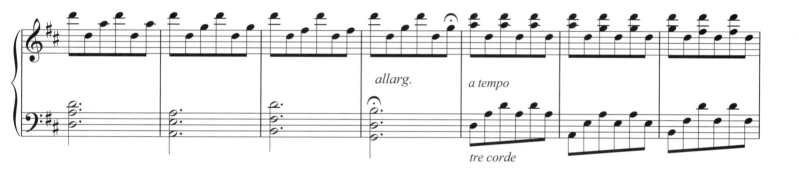

LA PLAGE

Words and Music by
YANN TIERSEN

Moderately fast

With pedal

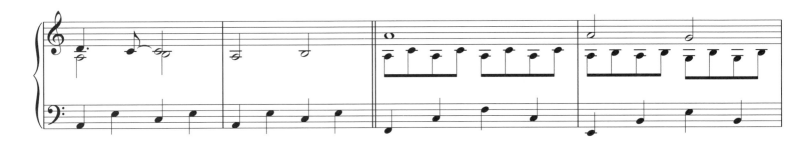

Copyright © 2005 by Universal Music Publishing MGB France
All Rights Administered in the U.S. and Canada by Universal Music - MGB Songs
International Copyright Secured   All Rights Reserved

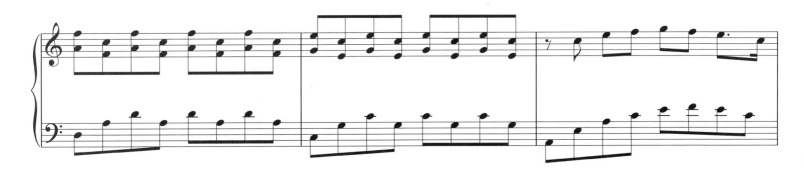

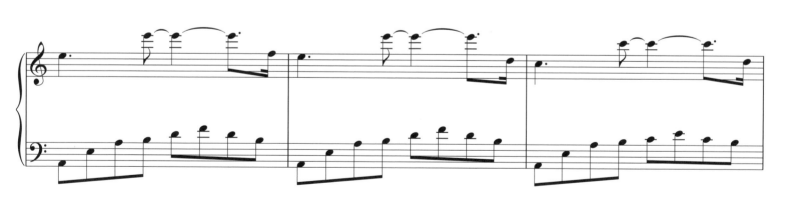

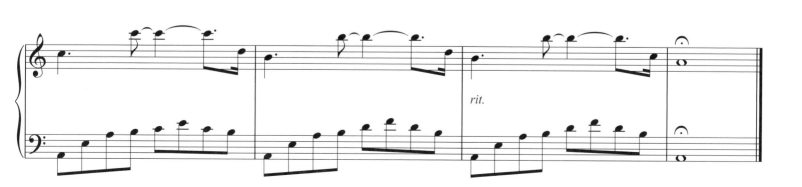

rit.

LOVE

By DAVID FOSTER

Copyright © 2020 by Fozbeats Music
All Rights Administered by Peermusic III, Ltd.
International Copyright Secured   All Rights Reserved

Freely (♩ = 60)

In tempo (♩ = 57)

Freely (♩ = 60)

LOVE'S RETURN

By DAVID LANZ

Gently, with freedom

Copyright © 2013 by Moon Boy Music (BMI)
All Rights Reserved   Used by Permission

(R.H. over)

dim.

Passionate

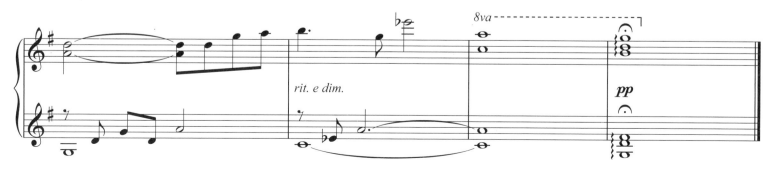

A MOMENT LOST

By DAVID NEVUE

Slowly, expressively (♩ = c. 60–84)

Very expressively (♩ = c. 80–96)

Faster, very freely

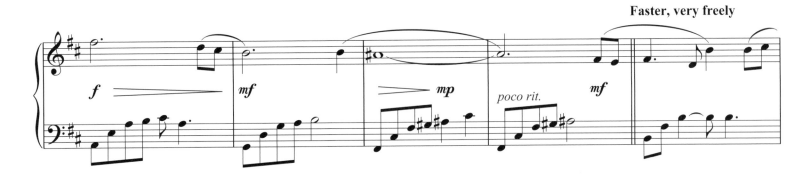

Copyright © 2005 by David Nevue
All Rights Reserved   Used by Permission

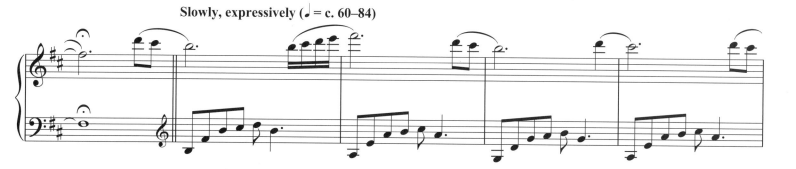

Slowly, expressively (♩ = c. 60–84)

Faster, very freely

74

Heavily (♩ = c. 80)

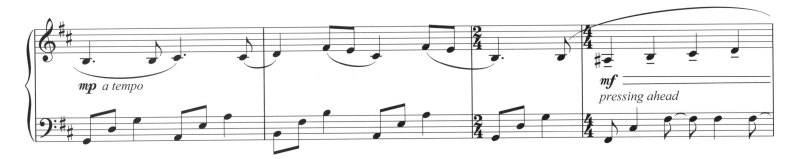

Slowly, expressively (♩ = c. 60–84)

MOMENTS

By ALEXIS FFRENCH

With tenderness and freedom

Copyright © 2018 UNIVERSAL MUSIC PUBLISHING LIMITED
All Rights in the U.S. and Canada Administered by UNIVERSAL - POLYGRAM INTERNATIONAL PUBLISHING, INC.
All Rights Reserved   Used by Permission

A NEW BEGINNING

Music by
PATRICK HAMILTON

Copyright © 2020 BROMO MUSIC PUBLISHING
All Rights for the World excluding Belgium Administered by UNIVERSAL - SONGS OF POLYGRAM INTERNATIONAL, INC.
All Rights Reserved   Used by Permission

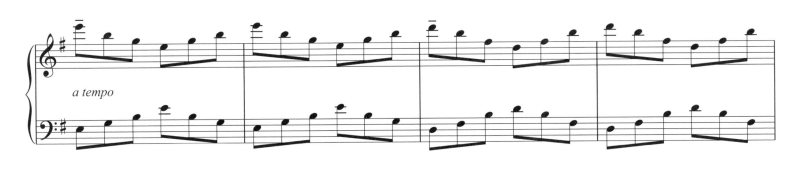

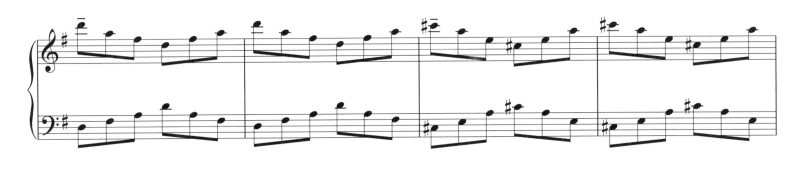

NOCTURNE IN A MINOR

Written by
CHAD LAWSON

Copyright © 2011 by Chad Lawson
All Rights Reserved   Used by Permission

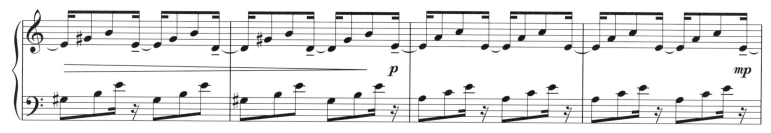

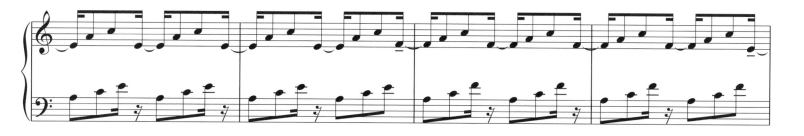

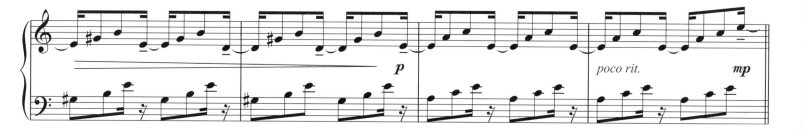

Slower (♩. = c. 57)

Faster, as before (♩. = c. 66)

Slowly, freely

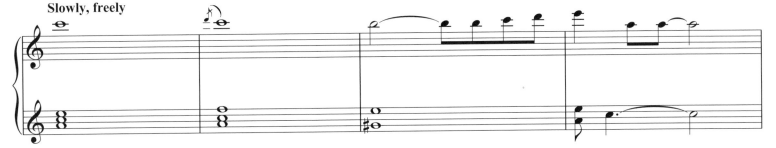

Slowly (♩ = c. 50)

p poco a poco accel.

Flowing (♩ = c. 72)

poco a poco accel. *mp*

Swiftly flowing (♩ = c. 144)

poco a poco rit.

Steadier (♩ = c. 120)

mf

mp poco accel.

poco rit. *mf* *poco accel.*

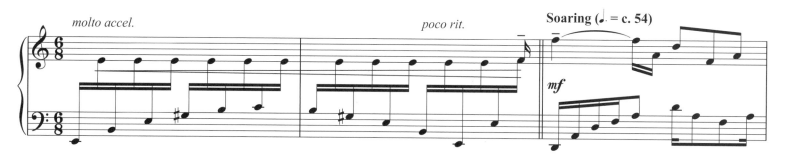

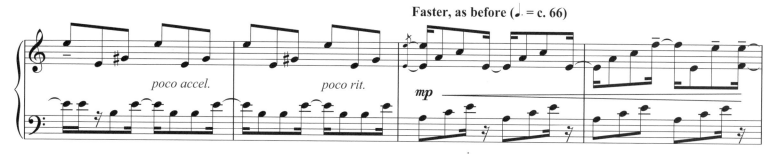

Slightly faster (♩. = c. 69)

poco accel.

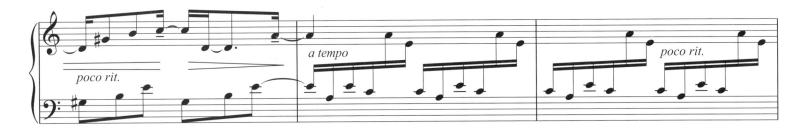

poco rit. *a tempo* *poco rit.*

Soaring (♩. = c. 54)

ten.

mf

poco rit.

Slowly, freely

8va

mp
molto rit.
p

RENAISSANCE WALTZ

By STELIOS KERASIDIS

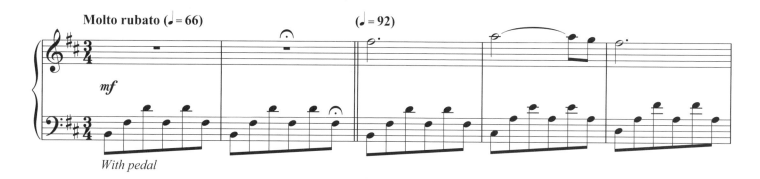

Copyright © 2021 by Stelios Kerasidis
All Rights Reserved   Used by Permission

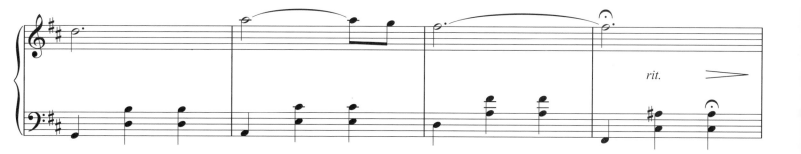

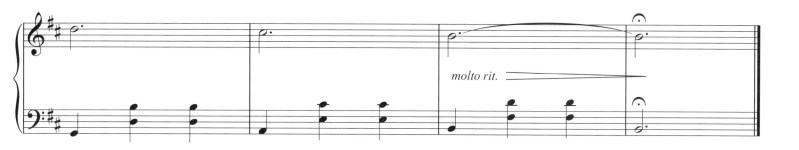

PORTUGUESE LOVE THEME

from LOVE ACTUALLY

Words and Music by
CRAIG ARMSTRONG

Copyright © 2003 UNIVERSAL PICTURES MUSIC
All Rights Controlled and Administered by UNIVERSAL MUSIC CORP.
All Rights Reserved   Used by Permission

Faster

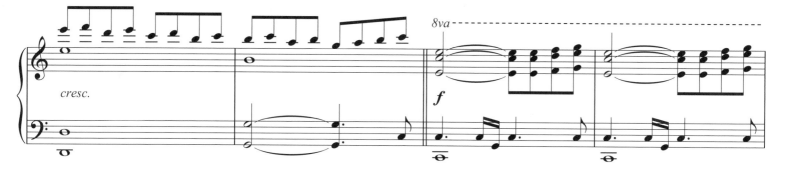

Slowly

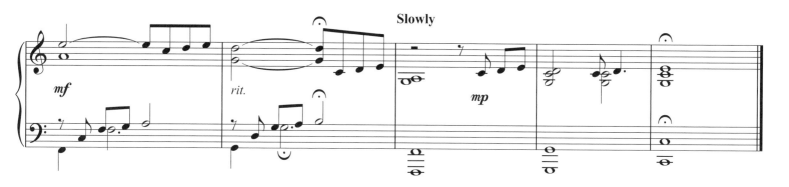

PORZ GORET

By YANN TIERSEN

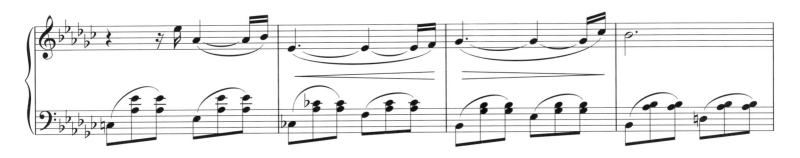

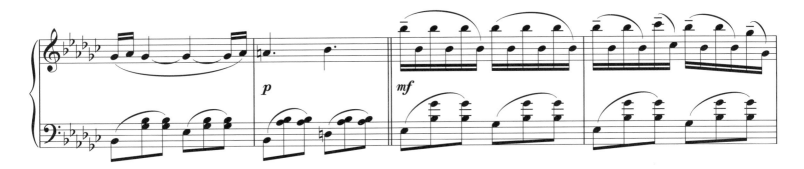

Copyright © 2016 Everything's Calm
All Rights Administered by Sony Music Publishing LLC, 424 Church Street, Suite 1200, Nashville, TN 37219
International Copyright Secured   All Rights Reserved

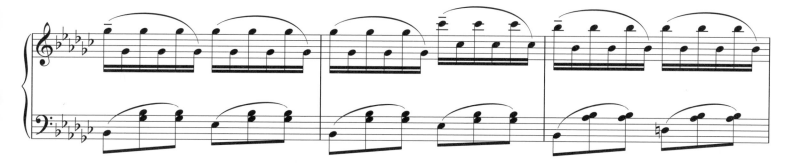

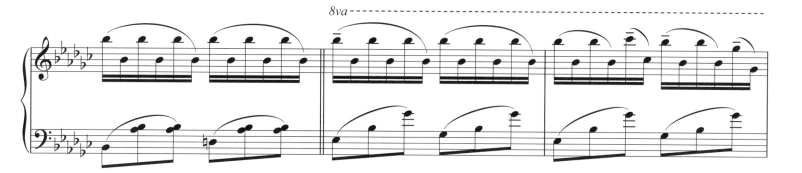

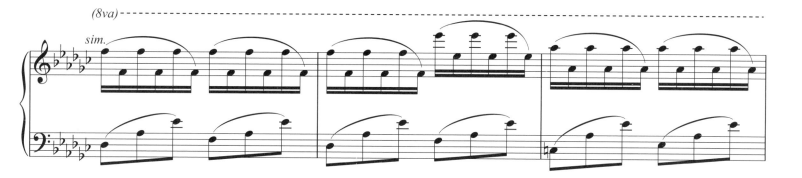

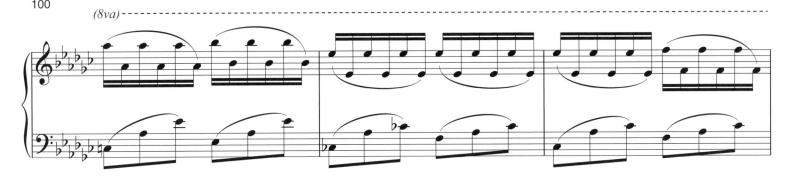

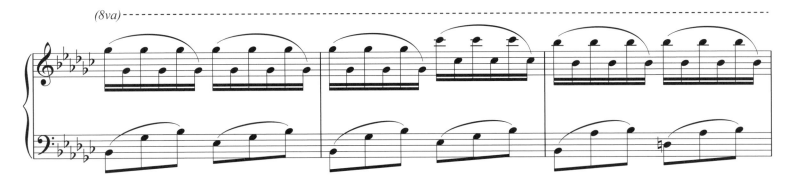

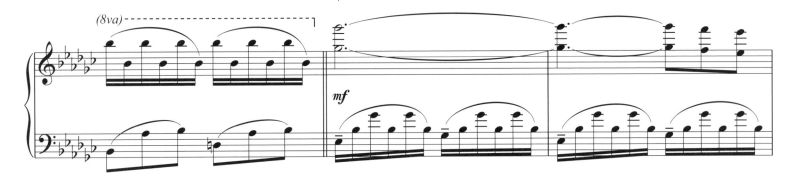

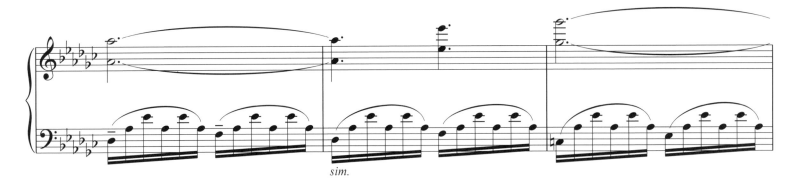

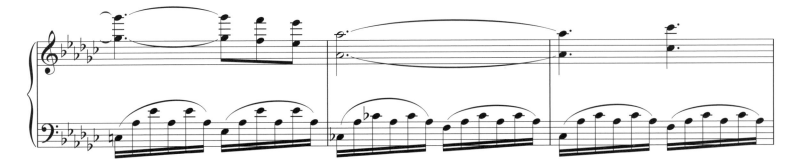

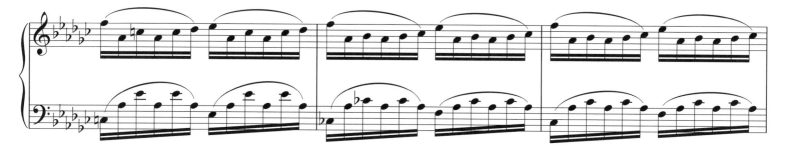

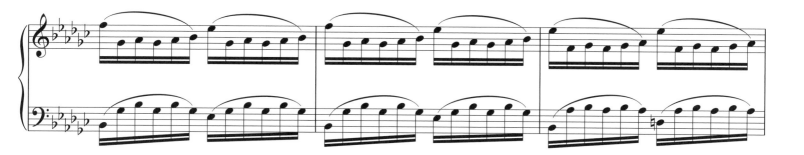

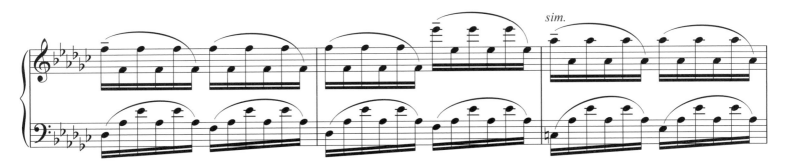

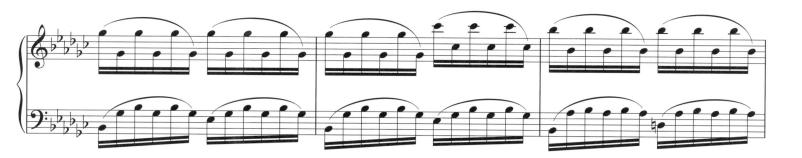

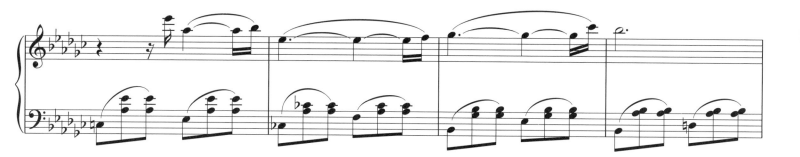

ROMANCES

Music by DAVID LINDGREN ZACHARIAS,
OLOF CARL JOHAN OLSON, EMANUEL OLSSON,
ERIK HOLMBERG and ANDERS PETTERSON

Copyright © 2017 UNIVERSAL MUSIC PUBLISHING AB, COSMOS MUSIC PUBLISHING, ERIK HOLMBERG PUBLISHING DESIGNEE and ANDERS PETTERSON PUBLISHING DESIGNEE
All Rights for UNIVERSAL MUSIC PUBLISHING AB in the U.S. and Canada Controlled and Administered by UNIVERSAL - POLYGRAM INTERNATIONAL PUBLISHING, INC.
All Rights for COSMOS MUSIC PUBLISHING Administered by CONCORD MUSIC PUBLISHING
All Rights Reserved   Used by Permission

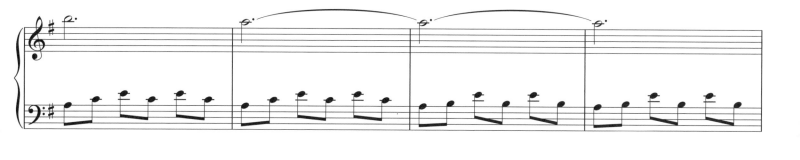

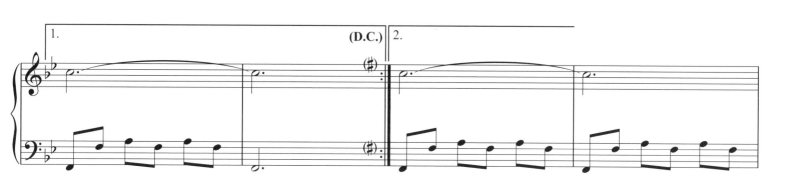

SEA CHANGE

By STEPHAN MOCCIO

Poetically and inspired

With pedal

Copyright © 2020 SING LITTLE PENGUIN
All Rights Administered by SONGS OF UNIVERSAL, INC.
All Rights Reserved   Used by Permission

SONG FOR SIENNA

Written by
BRIAN CRAIN

Courtesy of TuneCore Publishing o/b/o Brian Crain Publishing
All Rights Reserved   Used by Permission

SEPTEMBER SONG

Words and Music by
AGNES OBEL

Flowing, in 2

Copyright © 2013 UNIVERSAL MUSIC PUBLISHING LTD.
All Rights Controlled and Administered by UNIVERSAL - POLYGRAM INTERNATIONAL TUNES, INC.
All Rights Reserved   Used by Permission

116

To Coda ⊕

rit.

a tempo

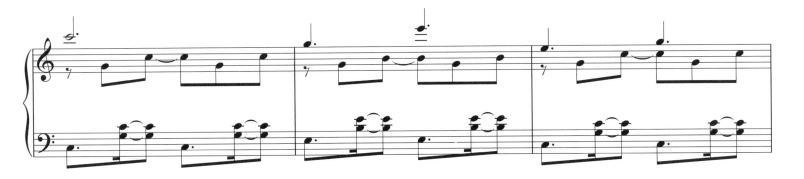

D.C. al Coda

rit.

CODA

rit.

SERENITY

By DAVID FOSTER

Copyright © 2020 by Fozbeats Music
All Rights Administered by Peermusic III, Ltd.
International Copyright Secured   All Rights Reserved

STILL
from NIGHT

Music by
OLA GJEILO

With pedal, una corda

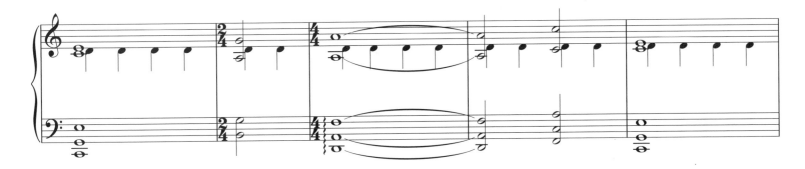

Copyright © 2019 Chester Music Limited
International Copyright Secured All Rights Reserved
Used by Permission

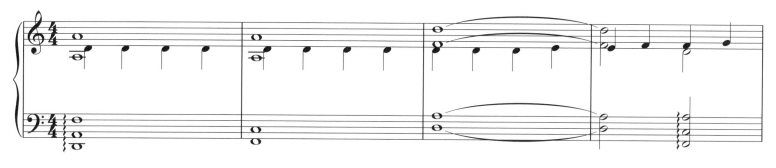

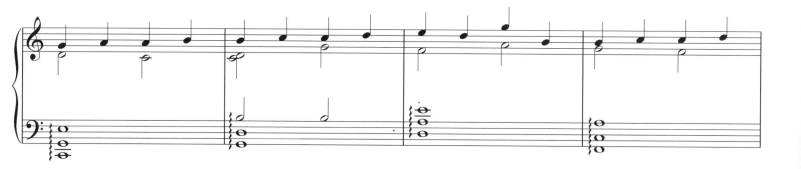

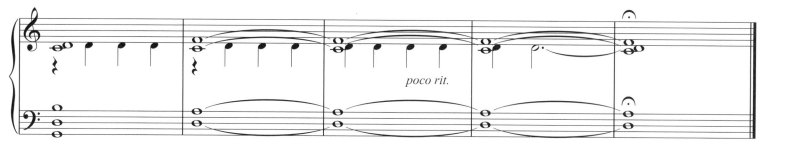

poco rit.

UNA MATTINA

Music by
LUDOVICO EINAUDI

Copyright © 2004 by Chester Music Limited
This arrangement Copyright © 2019 by Chester Music Limited
International Copyright Secured   All Rights Reserved
Used by Permission

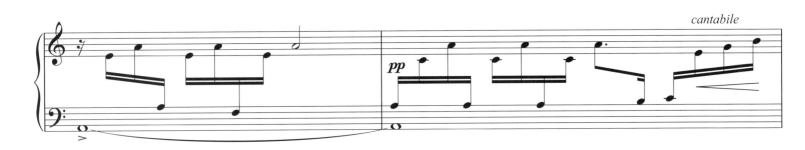

WHEN MORNING COMES

By PAUL CARDALL

Slowly, in 2

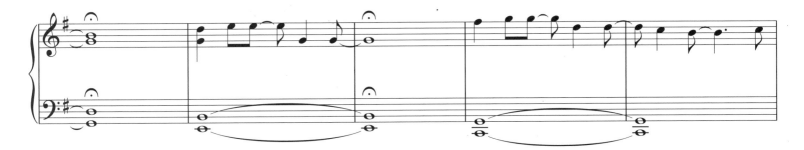

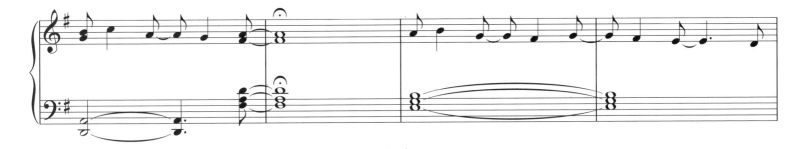

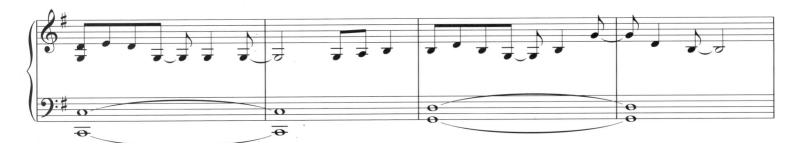

Copyright © 2019 Anthem Music Publishing I and Worth Of Souls Publishing
All Rights Administered by Anthem Entertainment
All Rights Reserved   Used by Permission

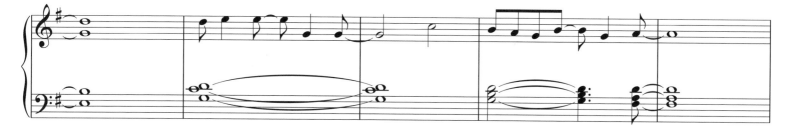

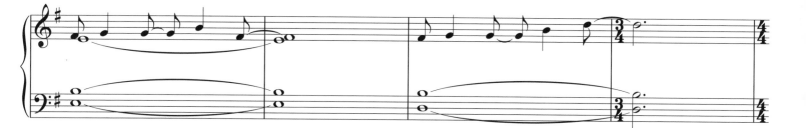

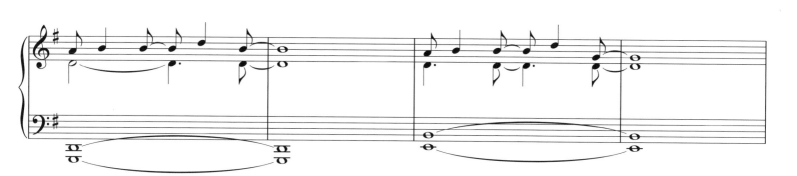

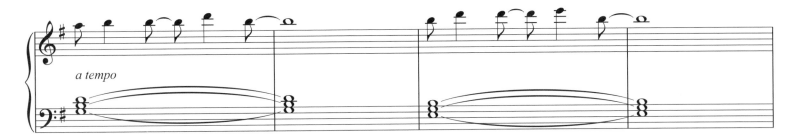

WINGED MELANCHOLY

Music by
PATRICK HAMILTON

Sweet and gentle with some rubato

Copyright © 2021 BROMO MUSIC PUBLISHING
All Rights for the World excluding Belgium Administered by UNIVERSAL - SONGS OF POLYGRAM INTERNATIONAL, INC.
All Rights Reserved   Used by Permission

25

WRITTEN ON THE SKY

Composed by
MAX RICHTER

Poco più mosso

With pedal

Copyright © 2004 Mute Song Limited
International Copyright Secured   All Rights Reserved

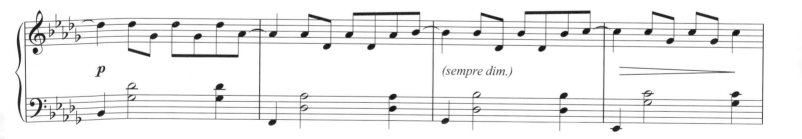

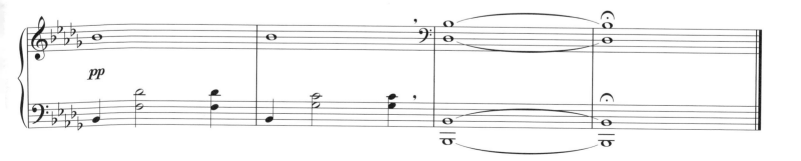

YOUR FAVORITE MUSIC
ARRANGED FOR PIANO SOLO

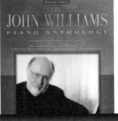

ARTIST, COMPOSER, TV & MOVIE SONGBOOKS

**Adele for Piano Solo –
3rd Edition**
00820186.............................$19.99

The Beatles Piano Solo
00294023.............................$17.99

**A Charlie Brown
Christmas**
00313176.............................$19.99

**Paul Cardall –
The Hymns Collection**
00295925.............................$24.99

Coldplay for Piano Solo
00307637.............................$17.99

**Selections from
Final Fantasy**
00148699.............................$19.99

**Alexis Ffrench – The
Sheet Music Collection**
00345258.............................$19.99

Game of Thrones
00199166.............................$19.99

Hamilton
00354612.............................$19.99

**Hillsong Worship
Favorites**
00303164.............................$14.99

How to Train Your Dragon
00138210.............................$22.99

Elton John Collection
00306040.............................$24.99

La La Land
00283691.............................$14.99

John Legend Collection
00233195.............................$17.99

Les Misérables
00290271.............................$22.99

Little Women
00338470.............................$19.99

Outlander: The Series
00254460.............................$19.99

**The Peanuts®
Illustrated Songbook**
00313178.............................$29.99

**Astor Piazzolla –
Piano Collection**
00285510.............................$19.99

**Pirates of the Caribbean –
Curse of the Black Pearl**
00313256.............................$22.99

Pride & Prejudice
00123854.............................$17.99

Queen
00289784.............................$19.99

John Williams Anthology
00194555.............................$24.99

George Winston Piano Solos
00306822.............................$22.99

MIXED COLLECTIONS

**Beautiful Piano
Instrumentals**
00149926.............................$19.99

**Best Jazz
Piano Solos Ever**
00312079.............................$24.99

Best Piano Solos Ever
00242928.............................$22.99

**Big Book of
Classical Music**
00310508.............................$24.99

Big Book of Ragtime Piano
00311749.............................$22.99

Christmas Medleys
00350572.............................$16.99

Disney Medleys
00242588.............................$19.99

Disney Piano Solos
00313128.............................$17.99

Favorite Pop Piano Solos
00312523.............................$16.99

Great Piano Solos
00311273.............................$19.99

**The Greatest Video
Game Music**
00201767.............................$19.99

Most Relaxing Songs
00233879.............................$19.99

**Movie Themes
Budget Book**
00289137.............................$14.99

**100 of the Most Beautiful
Piano Solos Ever**
00102787.............................$29.99

100 Movie Songs
00102804.............................$32.99

Peaceful Piano Solos
00286009.............................$19.99

**Piano Solos for
All Occasions**
00310964.............................$24.99

**River Flows in You &
Other Eloquent Songs**
00123854.............................$17.99

Sunday Solos for Piano
00311272.............................$17.99

Top Hits for Piano Solo
00294635.............................$16.99

HAL•LEONARD®

View songlists online and order from your
favorite music retailer at
halleonard.com

*Prices, content, and availability subject
to change without notice.*

Disney characters and artwork TM & © 2021 Disney